Walking My Road of Grief

Walking My Road of Grief

MATTHEW RUCKER

The Mulberry Books, LLC.

ISBN: 978-1-950850-28-0   [Paperback Edition]
        978-1-950850-29-7   [Hardback Edition]
        978-1-950850-30-3   [eBook Edition]

Printed and bound in The United States of America.

Published by
The Mulberry Books, LLC.
8330 E Quincy Avenue, Denver CO 80237
themulberrybooks.com

Contents

CHAPTER ONE
Getting To Know Brandon

CHAPTER TWO
My Road of Grief

ACKNOWLEDGEMENTS

Let me thank all of family, friends, and church members for being there for me. I particularly want to thank my friend and doctor, Doctor Michael Willmot, who was a Godsend. I would also like to thank my good friend, Billy Robinson, for the picture on the cover of the book. Each of you put your hand under me and lifted me up, but most of all I thank God for the mystery of these poems.

This book is dedicated to my deceased son,

Brandon Scott Rucker

who gave me thirteen great years

INTRODUCTION

My son committed suicide, at the age of thirteen, on January 25, 1995. This was by far the hardest lick life has hit me with. Yet my son prepared me as best he could for his death. I missed the signs at the time.

I remember after a young lady's funeral, Brandon made the statement, "Dad that was a cool funeral. I want you to promise me to do my funeral when I die". I remarked, "You will see me die first." He insisted that I promise him if something happened, I would do his funeral and I agreed.

He also prepared me the day of his death. I took him to school and as he got out, he turned and said, "Dad you know I love you?" I told him, "I love you too." He said, "Dad, no matter what happens, know that I love you." I said, "Okay". And he then replied, "You're a cool dad". Those were the last words on this earth that I heard from my son. That afternoon he was dead.

I said all of this to come to the book. The book consists of the time frame following his death. Now the mystery is the poems. I have never written poems before, so all of this is a mystery to me.

The poems would come all at once. The title first, then the poem and most of them came during the night. I would be awakened with verses running wild in my brain. Grabbing a pen and paper I would write as fast as I could. When I was through, I was physically and emotionally exhausted. I never had a clue to when they would come.

Now this book is written within the arena of feelings. I know facts about his death, but I concentrated on the feelings. Knowing all the facts doesn't ease the pain. I will not point the finger at anyone for each of us involved must take responsibility for our actions. God will be our final judge. So, stay with me with feelings as we walk together, my road of grief.

But first of all, I would like to introduce you to Brandon with some short stories. These are stories that involved him and paint a picture of what he was like.

CHAPTER ONE

Getting To Know Brandon

My Son's Birth

Brandon was born on October 15, 1981 at Darlington Hospital in Darlington, South Carolina. He was born just a stone's throw from the Darlington Racetrack where the Southern Five Hundred is run every year.

We arrived at the hospital and waited on his arrival. Now he wasn't like his sister. Brandon was ready to enter this world. Everyone was ready for his arrival. The doctor said, "He's got the head of a girl," but then he came out and the doctor held him up for us to see. About that time a stream of water hit the doctor between the eyes, and he replied, "He may have the head of a girl but a bottom that is all boy".

It was then I began to realize that he was going to be a rascal.

Growing up in Church

Both my kids grew up in the church. They were involved in Sunday School, Bible School and Morning Worship. They were both acolytes in the morning worship service.

Brandon developed his personal faith and joined the church at thirteen. He was one of those people who asked the hard questions about faith. We had some interesting talks, but his faith was always solid.

He always wanted to help someone usually from school. His world was not just about him but of others. That spirit continued to grow in him. He had a faith for living and he also had a faith for dying.

For that faith, I am proud of my son.

Christmas Time

This was an exciting time of the year. Decorations had to be put in the yard, and we had to go and select a Christmas tree for the house. Coming home we decorated the tree.

When Brandon and Rachael were small, Christmas Eve was a time of excitement. They didn't want to go to bed but finally agreed. My office was on the other end of the house, so I had a plan.

I would sneak out with a small bell and go to Brandon's bedroom window. "Tingle. Tingle." and then I would run back in the house to the office. Both of them would bust into my office eyes wide open saying, "We heard him daddy, we heard the Santa's bells". I would play with them saying, "Are you sure"? They would get excited trying to convince me that the bells were tingling. I would say, "Well, he must be close so go back to bed". Oh, the excitement of a little child at Christmas.

Good Student

Brandon enjoyed school and his grades reflected it. He loved all courses, but writing was inherited from me. I could read it, but the teachers had a hard time. He would tell them, "I write like my dad".

He could do his homework in a flash to go outside and play. What he really loved was to draw and he was good at it. His drawing consisted of all kind of things from the simple to complex.

When he was twelve years old, he told me he wanted to go to Clemson University and When he was twelve years old, he told me he wanted to go to Clemson University and become an architect. That became his goal to study and do well in school.

That awesome grin of his awarded him the teacher's pet in school.

A Country Boy

Brandon always loved going to the farm, my birthplace, to see Nanny and Pa. It was wide open space to run and explore. There were always the animals to feed or do something in caring for them.

My dad, Pa, always had something to do such as: feed the chickens, gather the eggs, and feed the cows and hogs. Dad would take time to explain things to him that he was able to use later on.

Brandon and I were the last two family members to see dad alive in the Lexington Hospital. It was a great visit and just three hours later Dad died with a blood clot.

Now when we would come to the farm, Brandon would always tell me, "I miss Pa". Yet the farm still pulled at him and his love never diminished, but only increased.

You see, Brandon became a farm boy longing to leave the big city and going to the country.

Matthew Rucker

Go-Kart Racing

Brandon went through the phase of racing. I bought the kids a go-kart and all the safety equipment. The helmet was one of the most important pieces for safety.

He and the next-door neighbor, would race on a track in a field between the two houses. It was about a quarter mile track.

Now Brandon would become a dare devil to win. On one particular day that I recall, as the two boys were coming around the curve, Brandon tries to pass and runs up on the wheel of Chad's kart and flips. The go-kart lands on his head and I do a record sprint over to him and lift the kart off him. He jumps up and takes off his helmet and says, "Dad that was so cool". Here I am standing here about to have a heart attack and he says, "Dad that was so cool".

I compose myself and try to explain some safe driving rules but it didn't help. When he got the dirt bike, there was only one speed which was wide open.

The Deer Hunt

When Brandon was six or seven he wanted to go deer hunting with me. I bought him a "BB" gun because of course he wanted a gun. He was excited about shooting a deer. Now friends a "BB" gun will not hurt a deer, but not in Brandon's mind.

We went to the deer stand and I knew a big buck (male deer) was in the area. So we climbed up into the stand to wait. I don't know how many questions he asked but it was a lot. "Dad do you see one yet? What time is it? Do you think one will come out?" I tried to keep him quiet but he hadn't learned to whisper.

All of a sudden I glimpsed movement to my right.

There the big buck was slipping into the field. Slowly I raised my gun when all of a sudden I heard "pop". The deer took off and Brandon stood up and shouted, "I hit him. Let's go get him". He was starting to climb down out of the tree as he was talking. Brandon exclaimed, "Let's look for blood because I hit him!"

I knew then that there would be no blood, but we looked anyway. I didn't have the heart to tell him the truth as excited as he was. You know I never got the opportunity to shoot that deer but Brandon's story lived on.

Fishing on the Lake

As I said in earlier stories, Brandon loved to fish. When he came to live with me and the weather was clear, we went fishing after church. I know some people will call me a heathen for going fishing, but I had just finished teaching Sunday school and preaching.

So we would hook the boat up Saturday, go to the store for snacks, drinks and ice. After I had told everyone "good-bye" as they left the church it was time to hit the lake. Next was locking the church and crossing the street to our home to change our clothes.

Getting in the truck we had one more stop, the chicken place for chicken, biscuits, fries and slaw.

Then off to the lake we would head.

After launching the boat we sought out a quiet cove to chow down on those fixings we had purchased. Then the time for fishing was at hand and we fished and talked.

My how I miss those times on the lake for those are precious memories. I would give anything to fish with Brandon again.

Loved Playing Football

Brandon always wanted to play football but he was small. I was afraid he would get hurt and yet each year he continued to beg me to play until I said, "alright".

My goodness he looked so small on the field but he played his heart out. He gave it 100% in practice never missing. In the game I would hold my breath when he was going to be tackled, but he always got up and be ready to go again. Brandon didn't have the size but he had the heart.

Every Friday night we had to go to the Woodruff High School game. He knew the players and would cheer them on. The coach who ended up in the South Carolina Hall of Fame, Coach Willie Varner, was a member of the church I served.

So at the end of each game while the TV cameras were rolling the coach would have his arm around Brandon talking to the media. Brandon was on camera every Friday night at the home or away games.

Coach Varner always told him "When you get to high school I'm going to make a safety on the team out of you". He was becoming a football player and loved every minute.

Brandon was Compassionate

Brandon was a giving child. At Christmas he would want to take some of his toys to give to others. He loved putting money in the Salvation Army kettles.

As he grew older he worked with my brother-in-law during the summer and on Saturdays sometimes. He always had money on him from working.

I remember picking up items at the store and realized that I had left my wallet at home after the cashier had totaled up our items. Brandon said, "Don't worry dad, I got it," and he paid the bill for the groceries. When we got home I tried to give him the money back, but he said, "No, I was glad I could pay for that". Christmas was a special time for him. He always wanted to have a white Christmas with snow. Brandon was very involved in the churches during this time with plays, parties, and visits church members' homes were just our norm.

I was so proud of my son's faith and how it helped him grow into the compassionate person he was.

Loved His Sister

Rachael and Bandon were joined at the hip. They did everything together. If she tried it, he had to try it as well. That got him into trouble at times.

They loved to fish and there were many happy days on the water. Both caught large striped bass and had to get them "stuffed" (mounted is the correct term). Boy did that trip cost me but each had their fish on the wall.

They loved to come to Nannies and Pa's house, my mom and dad's farm. Here on the farm they were free and with their cousin they explored a lot. Most of it was concerning the animals. Rachael, Brandon, and James would build pens, feeding, separating animals and other chores. They were free from the city and truly 'born free'.

Yes, they had some fights but always got over it quickly. They were very fierce when the other was threatened. In other words, they took care of each other. I must admit I had two great kids because they basically loved each other.

The Pain of Divorce

My divorce hit the kids and me hard. We were together as a family and now two families. I had to forgive my ex-wife for what she did but for the kids it wasn't that easy. My daughter still struggles today. Brandon being the sensitive one of the two took it hard.

My ex-wife gained custody of the children because I was training to be a Chaplain at Spartanburg Reginal Medical Center. When I completed the program I was assigned a church in Pelzer.

Brandon became so hard for my ex-wife to handle that she said, "He has to come live with you". So Brandon came to my house to live. Yet he brought some heavy anger with him for things he had seen at his mom's house. That anger never left him but he was happy being just with dad, yet missed his sister.

I made some big mistakes with my son at this time by forcing him to go to his mom's house. His anger was so great and if life had a reverse button I would have done things differently.

Even as I write I feel the emotions in my stomach for the divorce was pure hell for Brandon.

Bomb to Saddam

I got to know a jet fighter pilot of a F-15 who was stationed at the air base here in South Carolina. Brandon loved to fly and when he found out he had to meet him.

They struck if off and he told me to bring Brandon to the base. There would be passes at the gate on such a date for the visit. Brandon missed school and we headed to the base. Cliff was at the hanger and met us. Brandon thought it was so cool that, a military police escorted us to the hanger.

Since all this was top secret, security was high and it was exciting for him. We were then taken to a F-15 loaded and ready to take off, which was Cliff's plane.

A ramp was placed next to the jet so we could look down into the cockpit. Cliff pointed out various systems to Brandon and how he flew it. This was one of Brandon's greatest trips.

Cliff was deployed to Iraq and a few days later Brandon received a photograph showing a bomb on which Cliff wrote 'To Saddam from Brandon'. That bomb was dropped on the palace. Brandon proudly showed this to all his friends, a picture of the bomb dropped on Saddam for him.

Almost an Eagle Scout

Brandon joined the cub scouts and then when he was of age the boy scouts. Camping was his greatest love because we camped when we could, Brandon started in the living room under blankets over chairs to outdoor camping.

His favorite was when we night fished. Brandon would make his bed under the bow of the boat because there he was warm and dry. Now, I couldn't say that about me, but he loved camping.

He moved up in scouts and was working on becoming an eagle scout. There were various requirements and he was one step from being an Eagle Scout when he died.

What's interesting is that requirement came the very next day for Brandon from Senator Lindsey Graham. The Eagle Scout program was complete but a day late in his life. Yet in my mind he will be my little Eagle Scout. I am proud of you son.

Matthew Rucker

Almost a Black Belt

Brandon got into Karate at the age of eight. His teacher was Sam Chapman. He was a good student mastering each new level and gaining a new belt.

He was a participant in numerous shows but one of the biggest was the Battle of Atlanta. Brandon won the forms competition which he received a trophy that was taller than he was. He placed third in the sparing.

Now his practice partner was me but I had to stay on my knees when we practiced. He could kick and punch me but as his partner I could only punch.

It made his day if he could get a clean punch on me since I was a black belt.

As quick as he was I knew when he grew into the later teens he would have whipped me. Brandon would have gained speed while at my age I would have slowed down.

If he had lived I feel sure he would have achieved that goal in is life, a black belt.

Enjoying the Moment

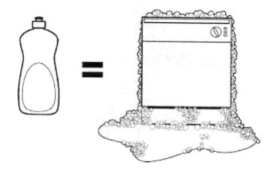

My mother-in-law got a new dish washer for Christmas. She loaded it with dishes and then for whatever reason she poured dish detergent in the cup holder. Two of her grandchildren were at the house that day when she started the dish washer.

In just a short while suds started coming out all around the door of the dish washer onto the kitchen floor. My mother-in-law was freaking out and the grands were trying to keep the suds from seeping out around the door.

Brandon, my wife and I came into the kitchen at that point in all of the commotion and excitement.

Standing in the suds on the floor, Brandon calmly exclaims, "This is so cool".

My wife shut the dish washer off and the grandchildren began having fun in the suds with Brandon. He enjoyed those little special moments of excitement.

Neighbor – Mr. Smith

Mr. Smith lived across the street from us. He was a grouchy individual that everyone stayed clear of. He could really hurt you with his words. About all I did was wave when I left home or returned, but I received few waves from him.

Now Brandon would go over to his house and help him in his yard. If he was raking leaves or picking up sticks, Brandon was there.

A vivid picture I have in my mind was the two of them pulling weeds out of the shrubbery. All you could see are two behinds next to each other facing the road. Brandon, in a sense became his family because he didn't have many of family to visit.

Now, Mr. Smith never visited our home, but when he heard of Brandon's death, he came over. Now this tough rough individual came into our home wiping tears from his eyes. I got up and hugged him and asked him to sit down.

Mr. Smith talked about Brandon, helping him and finally said, "You know the little rascal made me like him".

Now I hope from these stories that you can say, "I would have liked him too".

Brandon's Last Day

It was a cool Wednesday morning when we ate breakfast together. The date was January 25, 1995. I would take him to school and go to Columbia to take my mom to the eye doctor.

I told him that Harold, Angela's dad, would pick him up at school that afternoon. It would be late when I returned and Angela would be teaching a class after work.

Arriving at school before he got out he said, "Dad I love you". I told him, "I love you too". "No, Dad I want you to know that no matter what happens that I love you", Brandon responded. Then I remarked, "No matter what I love you". He continued by saying, "Dad, you're a cool dad and I love you". Those were Brandon's last words to me on earth that day.

I tried to call several times coming home but there was no answer. Brandon was probably playing with the neighbor's son whom he had done many times, I thought.

When I arrived at the house it was dark and as I walked through, I cut on the lights. Starting down the hall I noticed the computer room light was on.

When I entered the doorway, I saw him on the floor. It was like a bad dream. This can't be happening, it just can't be. I rushed to him, to try to revive him, blowing into his mouth I realized how stiff he was.

All I could think of was Brandon being alone, so I had to go to him. Taking my shotgun out of the closet I prepared to follow him. Placing the gun in my mouth thinking, I'm coming son. About that time the phone rang and that brought me back to reality and I answered the call. On the other end of the line was my wife, Angela, you see she saved my life.

Now, I was the chaplain for the police department, and they all came wanting to help in any way they could. I needed their strength at this time. The corner, I got to know as a Chaplain at Spartanburg Reginal Medical Center. It was as if God surrounded me with friends to support me and my wife.

Yet this was one of the worst days of my life, my last day with my son, Brandon.

CHAPTER TWO

My Road of Grief

The first poem came two days before the funeral. The promise I made to Brandon now weighed heavy on me. Doing his funeral felt impossible and I was numb. Dr. Michael Willmot came by the house and told my wife and I that he wanted to give us something to help us sleep. "You need your rest right now for the days ahead are going to be hard," he told us. We agreed so that night we took the pills and sleep came. Rhymes were running in my head and I tried to ignore them but couldn't. I got up and went to the desk. The title came first and then the words of which I wrote as fast as I could. After I finished, I was exhausted and went back to bed.

The next morning, I read what I had written. I couldn't believe I wrote a poem for I had never written one before. The poem was used on the bulletin for his funeral. By the way, the four years noted in the poem was him going to college. He planned to go to Clemson to become an architect.

So, I give you the first poem simply entitled "Goodbye", still a mystery of how it came.

Goodbye

I'm saying goodbye to my son today,
In a way that's so hard to say.

Thought I would say it as off to college he went,
Time away that would be well spent.

A degree to draw and architect you know-
Designing the future- I'm so proud I glow.

A good son he had always been,
Always loving to his friends and kin.

A smile to melt your heart, and a joke on his lips;
Why he had the whole world at his fingertips!

I thought four years it would be,
Not last Wednesday; Oh, Dear Lord, please help me

To say the words that sends him to his heavenly home,
And still his heart so no more he should roam.

Goodbye, my son, for you can't come to me;
But one day again, you I will see.

January 26, 199
Woodruff, South Carolina

The second poem came after the funeral when we all gathered at my mom's house with family and friends sitting around talking and laughing. I was sitting at the dining room table feeling so alone. The funeral was just a couple hours past and it is sad when you sit in a crowd and feel so alone.

Looking around the room I saw a picture of Brandon on the wall and that was the switch that turned my mind on. The verses began to come, and I tried to ignore them, but that was like telling your tongue to leave a sore alone in your mouth. Grabbing a piece of paper, a letter or something and wrote on the backside. Of course, the title is first and then the verses coming like a rapid machine gun. Finally, it was over, and I folded the letter up and put it in my pocket.

I was at peace and began laughing and talking with family and friends. After we left and went back to Woodruff, I read the poem. Here is what I wrote at the table at mom's a poem entitled "ALONE".

Alone

Tonight, I sit with you and feel so alone,
Missing my little buddy who has already gone.
I was doing real good trying to handle it all,
And then I saw his picture hanging on the wall.

I felt the pain and sorrow rising from deep inside,
And so I walked outside and just stood and cried.
Am I afraid to show you all my tears,
For missing my joy gone after just thirteen years!

I hear you talk of goats, food, and the road,
While feeling my soul crushing under my heavy load.
So hear me scream and hear me cry,
While I think, "Oh God, I just want to die".

Yet I'm glad you are with me, and please forgive my silent roar;
But my soul is bleeding, and I hurt to the core.
But I will stay with you, to laugh and try to feel swell,
And wait for God to give me the key to free me from this living hell.

January 28, 1995
Mom's house, Sandy Run, South Carolina

A good friend of mine is a counselor and he suggested my wife and I come to see him. He was very helpful and suggested we find a place alone where we felt close to God and write a letter to Brandon. Now I have always felt close to God in the mountains. There is something about the majesty and beauty that cries out God is here, especially when low clouds are present.

It was February so we headed to the mountains in Gatlinburg, Tennessee. Snow was on the ground and everything was so beautiful. The next morning we went to the chairlift and rode it to the top of the mountain to write our letters.

That night in the hotel room around midnight I woke up with a poem circling in my mind. Grabbing a pen and paper I wrote the poem "I Want to Die Today". It came at a very low point in my life and writing the letter triggered buried feelings.

I Want To Die Today

I didn't want to live anymore today,
For I felt living just wasn't the way.
Prayed to God to allow my soul to fly,
High, high up into the beautiful sky.

I didn't want to live anymore today,
For the past was good, but the present hurts more than I can say.
My heart is broken and it continues to bleed;
So emotionally weak, I feel death is what I need.

I didn't want to live anymore today,
So on top of the mountain I would pray.
Wrote you a letter to tell you how I feel,
For the counselor had stated that it helped to heal.

I didn't want to live anymore today,
For the pain is so great and nothing is okay.
Then God placed His hands around my broken heart as I did cry,
And said, "My child I'm with you, please try."

So Lord, I'm trying to live today,
Because you are with me along the way.
I still cry and feel so alone,
And the pain is so great, I hurt to the bone.

February 3, 1995
Gatlinburg, Tennessee

The fourth poem came the next night after "I Want to Die Today" poem. That poem left me at a low point in my life. I was down. Going to bed that night I tossed and turned but sleep came late. Around 1:30 am I woke up with rhymes running through my mind. Again, grabbing a pen and paper I wrote them down and fell asleep. It was the next morning when I finally read the poem. This poem was so revealing to me about what happened. I knew some facts but I never put them together. Once again, I don't know where this poem came from but I believe with all my heart this one was from Brandon. In my time of need he broke through. This poem helped me more than any of the others.

The poem talks about three key facts that I never put together. One was a scene he saw that caused great anger in him. The second were questions he asked me a few days before his death. He wanted to know how a person became gay. Were they born that way?

told him I didn't know but those who I counseled with seem to have some trigger such as: abusive mom, dad or molested by a family member were always brought up. I told him I didn't think you're born that way but I didn't know. The key is to love everyone as God said.

In conclusion, I'm not pointing fingers because everyone involved have to bear their own responsibility. What I am saying is that this poem got me up and going again. I give the poem that was given to me "My Son's Fear".

The third was a letter that I found after his death and I then knew why he asked the questions. It also explained the suicide note. You see I had not put them together until this poem. That's why I believe the poem was from him.

Matthew Rucker

My Son's Fear

Sometimes things happen in life we don't understand,
Like the mystery of life when a boy grows into a man.
The mystery brought feelings that changed from day to day,
That made you want to hide or just run away.

A scene from the past would come to you in sleep,
Waking you up, afraid that into the day it would creep.
A letter brought feelings of confusion that hid you behind locked doors-
Little did I know the questions that you asked were really yours.

How hard you tried to hide the truth from your friend,
Feeling if he knew, then that friendship would end.
How much you had to hide from all at school,
Covering your fear as a happy-go-lucky fool.

I really never saw this hurt and your awesome fear,
But how it must have tormented you over this past year!
From a boy to a man a journey you did dread,
The question of your manhood, gained from the lines you read.

February 4, 1995
Gatlinburg, Tennessee

Walking My Road of Grief

This poem was given to me two days later after arriving home to Woodruff, South Carolina. I guess what started it was the winding road through the mountains. I was tired physically and emotionally. I went to bed early. Around midnight I was awaken with the phrase in my mind: grief is a road over and over. Getting up I grabbed a pen and paper (by now I know the drill) and write as fast as I can. I finished it up and went to bed.

The poem talks of grief as a universal thing that hits us all. This road has highs and lows and not an easy walk. The road is wet from tears, yet it is a road we all must take.

This poem set me up for my walk that I was just beginning. It gave me insight of what was ahead. A poem given to me entitled "Grief is a Road".

Grief Is A Road

Grief is a road we all must take,
Filled with fears and feelings we can't fake.
Dark as the darkest night we ever did see,
Dear Lord, please walk the road with me.

Grief is a road that runs high and low,
Plunges us into valleys we could never know.
The pain cuts so deep we feel we will never heal,
Please, dear Lord, teach me how to kneel.

Grief is a road wet from many tears,
That flow from memories lost in future years.
A ruptured heart causes the fountain to flow,
Dear Lord, help me to see my pain that you know.

Grief is a road we all must take,
Filled with fears and feelings we can't fake.
Dark as the darkest night we ever did see,
Dear Lord, thank you for walking with me.

Woodruff, South Carolina
February 6, 1995

My walk of grief began with going back to the beginning, the night I found him. This poem came after midnight after I visited his grave. This was one of the longest poems. Waking up where phrases were swirling in my mind. Grabbing paper and pencil at my desk I began to write.

The poem starts with Brandon in bed. It then moves to him being on the couch. The key phrase is "daddy loves you". The scene of him sleeping carried through the years standing over him whispering, "I love you". My concern is that I wanted him to know that I loved him.

The poem switches to finding him in the room on the floor. My cry again was to say, "I love you Brandon".

I see the gun on the floor and at that time I didn't want him to be alone, so I would follow him. During this time I did sense a strange peace within my mind.

I got my gun and placed the barrel in my mouth. It was then that the phone rang and I came back to reality. My wife, Angela, had called me, saving my life.

The poem switches to seeing him in the casket and now telling him, "I love you, Brandon". The last stanza sees him in heaven and his words to me, "Daddy, I love you, I am right by your bed".

Now this poem really lays out the whole story. I read it the next morning and wondered how I could have written this poem. So I give you the poem, "I Saw You Lying There".

Matthew Rucker

I Saw You Lying There

I saw you lying there,
With your beautiful auburn hair.
I kissed you lightly on your forehead,
And whispered, "Daddy loves you," as I tucked you in bed.

I saw you lying there on the sofa where you had read,
Dreams of cartoons dancing in your head.
As I picked you up, your eyes opened for a peek,
And I whispered, "Daddy loves you, go back to sleep".

I saw you laying there, through the years the same scene,
Praying in my heart that you would know what I mean:
A love so strong, and oh, so deep,
I wanted you to know that before you went to sleep.

I saw you lying there with blood on your auburn hair,
Causing my heart to race, oh, what a scare!
I picked you up and held you close to me,
And whispered, "Daddy loves you, can you hear me?"

I saw you lying there, with gun in my hand,
For I would truly follow you to that promise land.
My heart was busted and my soul longed to take flight,
But a strange sort of peace consumed my fright.

God's awesome grace could not leave me alone,
Allowing me to hear the ringing of a phone.
My tears kept falling as rain from the dark skies

And I whispered, "I love you," as I looked into your eyes.

In a casket of black I saw you lying there,
Reaching out, I touched your beautiful auburn hair.
Bent down and kissed you as I had done all through the years,
And whispered, "Daddy loves you," through all the tears.

I see you standing there in Heaven so fair,
And at times I feel you, oh, so near.
Saying my prayers, I cover my head,
And I hear you whisper,
"Daddy, I love you, I'm, right by your bed."

After my visit to the Brandon's grave.
Sandy Run, South Carolina
February 9, 1995

Matthew Rucker

The seventh poem was written April 19, 1995 sitting home alone. My wife had taken her mom on a trip and this was the first time I had been alone in the house.

It was around 11 p.m. while sitting in the den that the rhymes started coming. I went to the office and quickly wrote them down. The setting when the poem started was in a dimly lit room as the poem brings out. Shadows were dancing on the wall and it was deathly quiet. I could almost sense his presence as memories cloud my mind. The poem is pretty straight forward except the line, "Three of us have gathered". I wondered about this for a while and then it came to me Brandon, God, and me. I give you the poem "Sitting Home Alone".

Sitting Home Alone

I sit alone tonight,
And the silence is almost deafening.
My stomach is nervous,
And the night feels threatening.

Shadows come alive,
And play with my mind.
Images on the wall,
Caress my heart and feel so fine.

I feel you, Son,
Look at the hair on my arm.
I sense your presence,
And feel no alarm.

I reach my hand out,
Touching the empty air.
For even though I can't see you,
I know your hand is there.

Matthew Rucker

Tears fill my eyes,
As I whisper your name.
Memories flood my mind,
In what seems to be a mental game.

As I sit in my chair,
The night rolls on.
Three of us have gathered,
And I don't feel so alone.

The eighth poem was written July 22, 1995. I was sitting at the kitchen table. It had been a while since the last poem. Drinking my coffee, a poem was the last thing on my mind. Then, it came all of a sudden, a phrase began running through my mind. The title came first then the versus. I wrote as fast as I could. It talks of missing him so and wondering if the pain will ever leave. Sometimes I could almost feel him in the den at night. So many memories in the town especially the school where I last saw him and the football field. The remembering brings pain because no more memories will be made. This poem states so much of what I am feeling. I give you the poem "I Miss Him So".

I Miss Him So

Oh dear Father, I miss him so,
Sensing his presence everywhere I go.
Will these tears from my eyes ever stop falling?
Will my broken heart ever his name stop calling?

Sitting in the den, I wait for him to walk through,
Full of energy, telling me of something we can do.
I walk out in the yard and look across the way,
Thinking that today with Brad he will play.

I drive slowly through our little town,
Sometimes crying like a sad-faced clown.
A trip by the school fills my eyes with tears,
As I see the field on which he played for two years.

My head tells me that to a better place he has gone,
And yet my heart quivers and feels so alone.
Will I ever stop feeling this gutting pain,
Or will it stay with me till we're together again?

The ninth poem came on Brandon's birthday after midnight. It was hard facing his birthday. He would have been fourteen. I tried to keep busy during the day with work. Yet night follows the day and sleep must come. I turned in early only to toss and turn. Sleep came late that night. Early morning I was awaken by the rhymes in my head. Knowing the routine I get up and write.

The poem talks of time that keeps moving. It talks of the present and the pain and sadness. Then it talks of the future and how the furthest I was from him was the day he died. Now with each passing day we are coming closer to being together again. The poem moves from sadness to excitement of being together again. I give you the poem "TIME MARCHES ON".

Time Marches On

Time marches on,
And I fight it from day to day.
Holding on to the present,
In such a desperate way.
Fighting Father time,
Not knowing what is ahead.
Fills me with feelings,
That I really dread.

Time marches on,
And I cry on certain days.
For the specialness of the time,
Removes my mind's haze.
And I can feel clearly,
As sadness erupts from my wound heart.
For today you will have been fourteen,
Only nine months since we did part.

But the furthest I was from you,
Was the day that you died.
While each day that now passes,
A new joy I feel inside.
For the nearer to my death,
The closer I come again to you.
To be together forever,
In a land beyond the blue.

So, time, keep on marching,
I embrace you each new day.
Holding on to the present,
But not in a desperate way.
I face Father Time,
With a faith for what's ahead.
With feelings of excitement,
And very little dread.

Matthew Rucker

It was 11:30 p.m. on August 17, 1995 and I was sitting alone in the suicide room. Visions of what I saw that night when I found him filled my mind. I think of suicide again and the peace I could find, but I couldn't do that because of Angela my wife and my daughter Rachael.

Then the rhymes begin, and I grab paper and pen and write. The title comes first and then I write as fast as I can. It's still a mystery of how this happens. The poem always seems to fit the situation and where I am emotionally. I was thinking about suicide and the poem lays it all out. It uses the characters "the Angel of Death", who is addressing me in gentle words. I listen because I can't go back, nothing is the same. I wonder how much I can take. The poem seemed to verbalize what I was thinking and feeling and brought it clearly to me. After reading the poem I knew I was going to live. How, I didn't know but I'm going to live. I give you the poem "The Edge of the Life/Death Line".

The Edge Of The Life/Death Line

The Angel of Death speaks softly,
To the pain in my mind.
Inviting me to find peace,
By crossing that life/death line.
I find it easier to listen,
As gentle words she speaks,
For death becomes the reality
Of what my soul seeks.

I sit and listen,
As my mind remembers when,
While realizing in my heart,
Those paths I will never walk again.
The sense of sadness overwhelms me,
As my heart continues to explode;
And I wonder how long it will be,
Before I fall beneath the load.

It's hard for me to get excited,
About the future and what's ahead.
For I feel no sense of joy,
My insides feel dead.
I wish I could say it's easier,
And that I'm doing fine;
But I sit here in my chair,
With a plan of suicide on my mind.

When does fantasy become reality?
And I walk across the line.
To find the inner peace,
That eases my troubled mind?
When will I not hear?
The gentle wooing voice.
That pulls me closer to death,
Of which I have no choice?

On January 8th, 1996 it snowed in Woodruff. Snow was always a high lite with me and the kids. We would build a snowman, go riding, and eat snow cream. It was an exciting time. But here I sit in my living room watching the kids play outside in the snow.

A wave of sadness fell over me because I wasn't playing. Sitting at the coffee table the rhymes started. Getting a piece of paper I write. This poem I must confess amazed me. It talked of the kid inside of me, that little boy. That little boy had died because he was connected to Brandon. I had a good cry after reading this poem "My Kid Died".

Matthew Rucker

My Kid Died

The kid inside of me died,
When I laid my son to rest.
Just going on with life,
Became an awesome test.
Fun things we did together,
Don't mean what they did before;
I felt each one leave,
As they walked out my heart's door.

When my kid died,
Fun no longer ran with me.
Feeling only emptiness,
I pretend, so no one can see.
Crying on the inside,
From sadness that eats my soul.
The past months I've not grown younger,
But, oh, I've grown so old!

Where is that kid inside of me?
Can he ever live again?
Or am I just dreaming,
My hope blinded by all the pain?
No, I guess I really realize,
That when it comes to fun,
Most of it was connected,
To my precious son.

Matthew Rucker

This poem was written before church on January 21, 1996. I would always sit in the office before I went out to preach. This was my quiet time. On this morning the phrases started running through my mind. I had two funerals that week and I think they figured into the mix. Grabbing a pen I wrote as fast as I could finishing when it was time to go out into the sanctuary for church. After the church service I took time to read the poem.

The first stanza talks about people dying and me saying words over them. It talks of wanting the same for me no more pain or sadness. The second stanza talks of wanting the sadness to leave. Two roads are before me and I'm not sure which would be best. The third stanza talks about my holding myself and whispering everything will be okay. All confusion will leave and the memories won't burn so bright.

That I will see clearly through the darkest night. Here then is the poem given to me "Sometimes".

Sometimes

Sometimes I envy people,
When they die upon the earth.
Finishing up their pilgrimage,
That they began at birth.
No more pain and sadness,
How attractive that can be!
Saying words over them,
Sometimes I wish it were me.

Sometimes I wish the scales of sadness,
Would fall from my eyes.
Letting me see my future,
That's clear without disguise.
To choose a path before me,
To know what to do.

Matthew Rucker

Fills me with confusion,
I stand blinded without a clue.

Sometime I want to hold me,
And whisper that everything will be okay.
That all my confusion,
Will one day go away.
The path before me will become clearer,
As sad memories don't burn so bright.
And I will see clearly,
Even through the darkest night.

January 25, 1995, was the anniversary of Brandon's death. Feelings were high during this time.

A few weeks before I had a dream about Brandon where he came to my living room to play once more which was so real. We wrestled on the floor and he tried to push me out the door. We had a good time and it seemed so real waking up I actually felt he had been there.

On the 25th I went to bed as always, tossed and turning a while. Sleep comes but after midnight I am awaken with the phrases and it is time to write. So again I grab pen and paper and the poem talks about dreams that come after midnight and how real they are. Some make me laugh and others make me cry. It also talks about the dream I had a few weeks before.

The poem relives the dream, wrestling and being pushed out the door. What was the meaning of this dream? The last verse clues it. In the Methodist Church we have to decide if we are moving from the church we are now serving. Memories were so powerful in this house and I debated back and forth whether to leave. I knew after this poem it was time to move. I give you the poem "Dream After Midnight" that led to my decision to move.

Dream After Midnight

Some dreams come after midnight,
They fade with the first rays of dawn.
While others sail into the day,
And live on and on.
Some are fresh as yesterday,
While others go back a lifetime.
Always riding with me,
Ever present in my awakened mind.

Some dreams make me laugh,
While others make me cry.
Filling me with understanding,
Yet still leaving me wondering why.
Such was the dream of my son,
That came a few weeks before.

A strange kind of visit,
If I were asleep I really don't know.

He came to me after midnight,
To play in our living room once more.
A smile on his face,
He tried to push me out the door.
After a time of wrestling,
He turned to leave the room.
Smiled, and said softly,
"Dad, I'll be back to get you soon".

The midnight dream not fading,
It exploded into the day.
So real I felt I touched him,
As again he came my way.
"Brandon, what were you trying to tell me?"
Remembering makes me both laugh and cry.
Maybe you wanted to tell me,
To leave the house in which you did die.

Matthew Rucker

This poem was given to me while I was sitting at the kitchen table at 12:30 a.m. I just couldn't sleep. The rhymes started so I wrote. It didn't take long to write at all.

This poem is kind of a gut check to see what I have left. Grief has taken so much from me. Laughter was always a part of my life but it has gone away.

Walking in silence is how I seem to respond to it all. The "sobs of sadness" are from the memories I have. Turning my eyes heavenward I look for relief, help from God. I am still leaning on Him. I give you the poem given to me "Sometimes I Walk In Silence".

Sometimes I Walk In Silence

Sometimes I walk in silence,
And listen to myself.
Try to put it all together,
To find out what I've got left.
Grief has really robbed me,
O feelings that energize.
Taking away my laughter,
And the sparkle from my eyes.

Sometimes I walk in silence,
And listen to what I say.
Hearing sobs of sadness,
From reminders that come my way.
The hurt in my gut is so great,
It brings forth a gentle groan.
Then I turn my eyes heavenward,
And feel my soul begin to roam.

Matthew Rucker

This poem came on my birthday, February 15, 1995. I was sitting up, my mind in gear, and thinking about the past. It was late and I fell asleep on the couch. Waking up my mind was racing with rhymes. Grabbing a pen and paper I wrote.

This poem begins with night coming and time for bed. Brandon and I are getting ready to walk down the hall. The hall is dark so he asks me to go first. This was always the scene.

The poem then moves to the question of life and death. The point being when it comes to death a daddy should always go first.

The last verse talks of Brandon's death. It occurred at night when shadows were falling. What he was facing pushed him over the edge. So in that quivering voice he said, "Daddy, I'll go first". So I give you the poem given to me "Daddy, I'll Go First".

Daddy, I'll Go First

When night comes softly,
And shadows begin to fall.
The time comes for my young son,
To begin walking down a dark hall.
He stops halfway,
Asks for water for his thirst.
Then with a quivering voice,
Says, "Daddy, will you go first"?

When night comes softly,
And shadows begin to fall.
Sometimes I lie awake thinking,
Of life and death, the mystery of it all.

We are given life on this earth,
As a blessing not a curse.
And when it comes to death,
A Daddy always should go first.

Matthew Rucker

So night came softly,
The shadows began to fall.
And the pain my son felt,
Pushed him toward some deeper call.
He stopped halfway,
His heart about to burst.
Then with a quivering voice,
Said, "Daddy, I'll go first".

On April 10, 1996, this poem came to me at 11 p.m. while I sat at the kitchen table. This was one of the most difficult poems to wrap my mind around. From the notes I wrote at the time my mind was hopping around from one thing to another. I wasn't sad or angry just laid back. I was getting ready to move from the church I loved but I knew that moving had to happen. This dominated my thinking. That's why this poem is hard to understand.

It talks of my mind wandering and taking me back to my grief. Now grief and anger run together. So the poem points that out. Grief and anger are the dominant themes that run through the poem. I guess it brings me back to what I had hidden by putting on a happy face. Grief and anger are still a part of my life. This is a mysterious poem for me the poem "My Mind Wanders".

Matthew Rucker

My Mind Wanders

My mind goes off wandering,
At times when I feel so low.
It digs up painful memories,
As off to an emotional hell we go.

Grief and Anger lie in wait,
As along memory lane we tread.
They hid in some Good Time's shadow.
The waiting is what I dread.

Then ambushed by a scene so powerful,
I feel my tears fall like rain.
Grief and Anger seize my broken heart,
And I wonder if I can survive the pain.

So, Mind, please stay with me,
And don't go wandering out by yourself.
Remember, Grief and Anger run together,
And if I lose you — I have nothing left.

This poem was written July 7, 1996, after midnight. I had now moved to my next appointment leaving the previous church behind. I believe this poem has something to do with this moving. Yet it's written in the context of Brandon's death.

The poem begins by asking the question "Do you still remember me". When you go to all the old places we used to go.

The poem switches and proclaims, "I remember you, for death can't keep us apart". There are those places of great memories and that keeps me alive.

I believe the poem gives healing to me and comfort in moving. If there is more I'm missing it. See what you think as I give the poem given to me "Do You Still Remember".

Do You Still Remember

"Do you still remember me,
Since I've been gone.
When only memory continues,
To live on?
Do you think of me,
When walking all alone.
In places that once,
We claimed as our own?"

"I remember you,
For death can't keep us apart.
I still hold you,
So deep within my heart.
I think of you,
And cry when alone.
And feel you so close,
In places we called our own."

This poem was given to me on July 23, 1996, at home after midnight. I'm not sure why this one came. It talks of dying and two directions after death. One leads to life or the other to a vast nothingness.

The poem points out that both paths are decided by death and no matter which one the pain is gone. I believe in life no matter what "Some People Say".

Matthew Rucker

Some People Say

Some people say,
When we die that's the end.
Forever lost in a vast nothingness,
Never to experience life again.
Some people say,
When we die life goes on.
In a land of peace and joy –
No more hurting to the bone.

Die to die,
Or die to live?
So confusing,
If some thought we give.
Who is right?
Who is wrong?
Only death gives the true answer;
Either way our pain is gone.

It has been sixteen months till the next poem comes on November 22, 1997. I have gone on with life holding on to my faith. This poem came after midnight, a cold rainy night. I'm not sure the meaning of this poem except telling me the grief is slowly slipping away. The fear seems to be leaving my life. I don't think it is so much about Brandon, but me.

The poem talks of a "time to die". Maybe it's telling me new life is coming in spite of all the problems. So I have to learn to love me and wait for the day for Brandon and I to be together. I will hold him one sunny day. Those are my thoughts as I write "Slipping Away".

Slipping Away

Dad, I'm slipping, slipping away,
Out into the dark night, leaving the bright day.

The darkness surrounds me; it seems to flood my soul,
My fear is leaving and I feel so bold.

The time for me to die has come to past,
The problems I face would always last.

So please just love me as I slip away,
And I'll hold you again one sunny day.

This was the last poem given to me after midnight on June 27, 1998. I didn't know it at the time but no poem has come since that night. It has been roughly 20 years. Nothing like this has ever happened to me again. What's interesting to me is that the first poem talked of goodbye to my son and this poem is also goodbye. The poems began with "Goodbye" ends in "Goodbye".

The poem talks about saying goodbye tomorrow hoping the dawn doesn't come quickly. The memories are still here but it's good to be alive and I'm ready for the future.

The last verse is saying "Goodbye" and I'm going to miss you. But I have brought you this far so you can continue your journey. A poem from the one who gave me the help in my walk of grief and hear are the words of goodbye in the poem "Tomorrow We Say Goodbye".

Tomorrow We Say Goodbye

Goodbye.
{ for now }

Night please pass by slowly,
Don't race to the dawn.
For tomorrow we say goodbye,
And I feel I can go on.

Memories of the past dance before me,
I see them in your face.
It's good to be alive today,
But for the future I must brace.

When we say goodbye tomorrow,
I don't know when you again I'll see.
But I know as this night passes,
A part of life dies within me.

EPILOGUE

In my profession as a minister I have seen suicide many times, especially as a Chaplain in a Trauma Center. From the old to the young they come through the emergency rooms.

When faced with a suicide I would always try to help the family the best I could. I would try to give them something to hold on to in their time of great sadness and anger. After a while with them I would try and explain the three questions people ask. The first is the question, "Why"? Somehow we question why it happened? Why did God let it happen? Why, why, why as if we know the facts it will make things better. Well, it won't. It won't ease the pain at all knowing all the facts.

Second comes the question, "What if? What if I had called or dropped by, what if"? I try to tell them that this was the victim's decision. You were not invited in. They made the decision; there was nothing you could have done.

The third question is, "What now? Where do I go from here? How can I go on?" This is where your faith comes in and healing begins. Now this doesn't come quickly, it takes time.

With the death of my son, I had to take my own advice. I asked those questions and now I can write about them. It took me twenty four years since his death and twenty years since the last poem. As I said these poems are still mysteries to me. I still don't know where they came from but I believe in my heart they came from God. Yes, I did ask the questions but the poems helped me in my walk of grief.

Matthew Rucker

One thing I tried to do was to capture the setting for each poem with what was going on in my life that day, the time the poem came, and other facts. Anything to try to understand what was going on. Even though I can write about them some years later, I'm still no closer to understanding the mystery.

I trust the poems will be meaningful to you the reader. I knew they were helpful to me. Maybe they can speak to you, especially in your walk of grief. I know I feel better after writing this book. May God bless each of you.

CPSIA information can be obtained
at www.ICGtesting.com
Printed in the USA
JSHW020229220720
6794JS00002B/60